**Bibliographic information published by the German National Library:**

The German National Library lists this publication in the National Bibliography; detailed bibliographic data are available on the Internet at http://dnb.dnb.de .

**Imprint:**

Copyright © 2015 GRIN Verlag, Open Publishing GmbH
Print and binding: Books on Demand GmbH, Norderstedt Germany
ISBN: 9783668187733

**This book at GRIN:**

http://www.grin.com/en/e-book/318292/the-renault-nissan-alliance-a-case-study

Nils Cröger

# The Renault-Nissan Alliance. A case study

GRIN Publishing

**GRIN - Your knowledge has value**

Since its foundation in 1998, GRIN has specialized in publishing academic texts by students, college teachers and other academics as e-book and printed book. The website www.grin.com is an ideal platform for presenting term papers, final papers, scientific essays, dissertations and specialist books.

**Visit us on the internet:**

http://www.grin.com/

http://www.facebook.com/grincom

http://www.twitter.com/grin_com

# Ramkhamhaeng University

Assignment for Course:  Management of Change and Development

Submitted by:  Nils Cröger

Date of Submission:  04.03.2015

Title of Assignment:  Case Study of Renault-Nissan Alliance

## Table of Contents

## Table of Figures

**Case Study of Renault-Nissan Alliance**

# Introduction

The story of Renault is first the story of a man with an unusual destiny. The adventure began on December 24, 1898. At this time Louis Renault took up a challenge to drive his A-type Voiturette up the steep Rue Lepic in Paris. Founded in 1898 by Louis Renault Voiturette, the company quickly became the leading industrial manufacturer in France. The mechanical, design and stylish innovation make it to a famous brand. Renault as a company has contributed immensely to the development of the automobile industry all over the world. The Renault company employs over 166.000 people across the globe with production plants in Europe and outside Europe (www.renault.com, 2015).

Nissan was jointly established in December 1933 in Japan as Jidosha Seizo Co., Ltd by Nihon Sangyo Co., and Tobata Imono Co. to manufacture and sell Datsun cars and parts. In June 1934, the company was bought by a new sole owner; Nihon Sangyo, who later changed the company's name to Nissan Motor Co., Ltd. The company works with manufacturing, sales and related business of automotive products, industrial machinery and marine equipments. The Nissan company employs over 133.000 people (Nissan facts booklet found on www.nissan-global, 2015).

Figure 1 shows the basic information about the two companies.

Figure 1: *Basic information about the companies*

| Car manufactures | RENAULT | NISSAN |
|---|---|---|
| Founding | 1898 | 1933 |
| Residence | Boulogne-Billancourt, France | Yokohama, Japan |
| CEO | Louis Schweitzer | Yoshikazu Hanawa |
| Sales number | 2.356.208 | 2.632.876 |
| Revenue | 40,2 Mrd. € | about 50 Mrd. € |
| Profit | 1,1 Mrd. € | about 2 Mrd. € |
| Number of employees | 166.114 | 133.833 |

Source: Own figure based on www.nissan-global.com, 2015; www.renault.com, 2015.

Since the beginning of the 1990's, Renault had been looking for a global partner. The reason was that the European market (Renault's major market) was increased. Moreover worldwide competition was fierce and growing customer demands and sophistication increased the pressure on car manufactures. In order to survive in this highly competitive and increasingly sophisticated industry, it became apparent that Renault needed a strong global partner to enable it venture into the international market. Nissan had often been cited as one of the best in Japan. It had top class engineers, which gave the company a unique capability and excellence in engineering and industrial quality. Moreover Nissan seemed to be the most global of all the Japanese carmakers since it was well established in Japan, the Americas and to a much lesser extent Europe. However the lack of focus on profitability and the Asian crisis had a negative effect on Nissan. They started to struggle to remain profitable for more than a decade. (Emerson, 2000).

Figure 2 shows the situation before the companies had the alliance.

Figure 2: *Basic information about the companies*

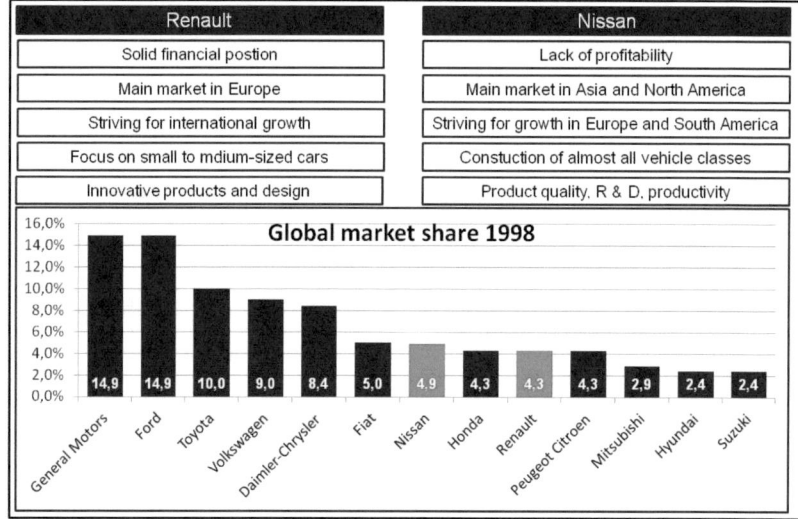

Source: Own figure based on Fagan & Yoshino, 2003.

The agreement establishing the Renault-Nissan Alliance was signed on March 27, 1999. It marked the first industrial and commercial cooperation of its kind between a French company

4

and a Japanese company, each with its own corporate culture and brand identity. Both companies were to share a common strategy of profitable growth and a community of interests. In order to reach this objective the Renault-Nissan Alliance established multiple joint projects, which covers most activities of both companies (Alliance booklet 2015). The cooperation within the alliance is about the most areas of the companies operations. This includes strategic management, purchasing, information technology, personnel exchanges and training as well as a number of collaborative ventures. Since 1999 joint structures have been introduced in Europe to rationalize distribution costs, share fixed expenses, improve the competitiveness of sales network and support the growth of Nissan and Renault. In 2010 the both companies (together) were the 4th largest automobile manufacturer in the world. But why was the alliance between two apparently very different companies/cultures so successful? To answer this question we have to discuss what is a strategic alliance in general and after that we try to find an answer with the methodology Organizational Development (OD)

## Strategic alliances – definition, motives and goals

The term strategic alliance has become widely used to describe a variety of different cooperation agreements ranging from shared research to formal joint ventures and minority equity participation (Susini, 2004). According to Ring (2000), an alliance involves the collaboration between two or more firms that retain their autonomy during the course of their relationship. An alliance is strategic when it has been design to enable the partners to pursue objectives that they have defined in the course of making decisions on the corporate level of business level strategies. The following figure 3 shows the motives and objectives why companies establish a strategic alliance.

Figure *3: Motives and objectives for a strategic alliance*

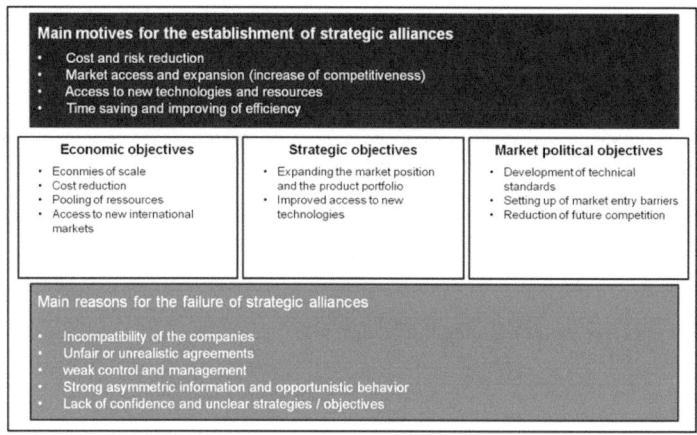

Source: Own figure based on Arino, Darcia-Canal & Valdes, 1999; Bamford, Ernst & Fubini, 2004; Kale & Singh 2009.

The main drivers for the establishment of a strategic alliance are competitive pressure on price, quality and technology, economies in capital investment costs and economies of scale and scope in purchasing, manufacturing, marketing and distribution.

The type of Renault-Nissan alliance is an unequal equity arrangement which is a mix of a competitive and intra-industry alliance since the two partners used to compete on the same range of products and of a noncompetitive agreement since Nissan and Renault are quite complementary as far as geographical market presence and market niches are concerned (Chanaron, 2007).

## Application of Organizational Development (OD) – Renault-Nissan Case

Before we start to answer the question: Why the alliance between two apparently very different companies/cultures was so successful? We analyze the situation before the alliance. For this purpose we use the SWOT analysis.

Figure 4: *SWOT analysis*

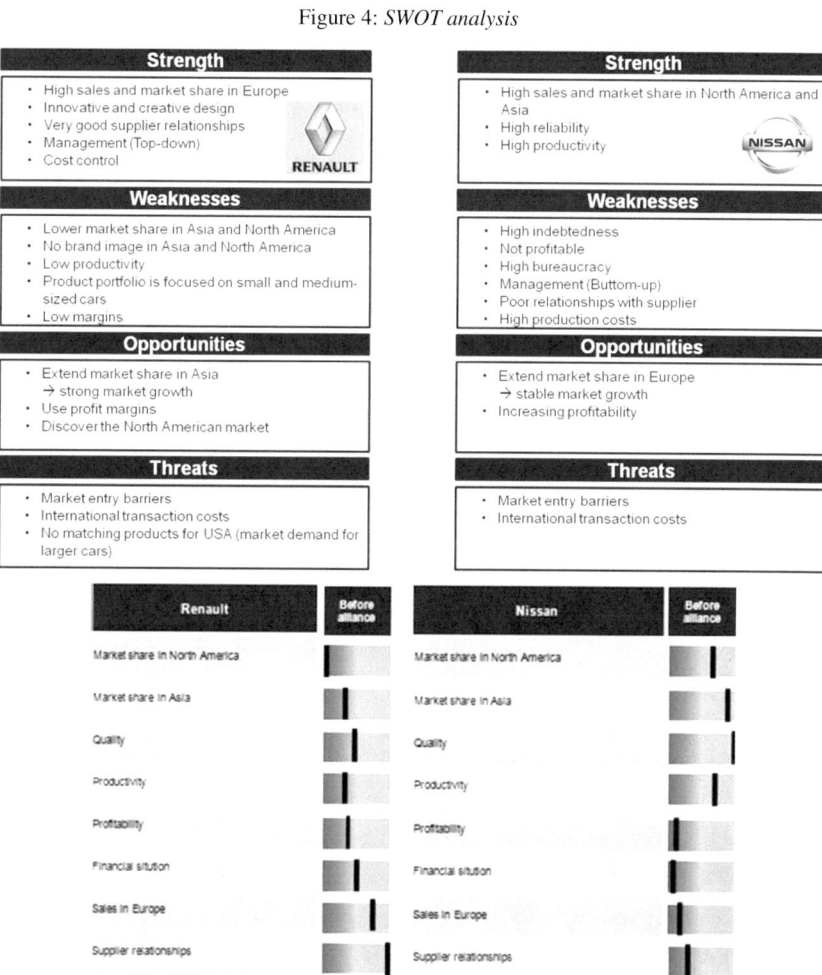

| Strength |
| --- |
| • High sales and market share in Europe<br>• Innovative and creative design<br>• Very good supplier relationships<br>• Management (Top-down)<br>• Cost control |

| Weaknesses |
| --- |
| • Lower market share in Asia and North America<br>• No brand image in Asia and North America<br>• Low productivity<br>• Product portfolio is focused on small and medium-sized cars<br>• Low margins |

| Opportunities |
| --- |
| • Extend market share in Asia<br>→ strong market growth<br>• Use profit margins<br>• Discover the North American market |

| Threats |
| --- |
| • Market entry barriers<br>• International transaction costs<br>• No matching products for USA (market demand for larger cars) |

RENAULT

| Strength |
| --- |
| • High sales and market share in North America and Asia<br>• High reliability<br>• High productivity |

| Weaknesses |
| --- |
| • High indebtedness<br>• Not profitable<br>• High bureaucracy<br>• Management (Buttom-up)<br>• Poor relationships with supplier<br>• High production costs |

| Opportunities |
| --- |
| • Extend market share in Europe<br>→ stable market growth<br>• Increasing profitability |

| Threats |
| --- |
| • Market entry barriers<br>• International transaction costs |

NISSAN

Source: Own figure.

These figures show that the strength of the one company is the weakness of the other company. They complement each other perfectly. But there were also restraining forces like the different language or coordination problems.

Figure 5: *Force field diagram*

Source: Own figure.

We have two companies from two different countries. They do not share a common language and therefore to communicate effectively is not easy. So both learned a common language, in this case English. Also the Japanese work culture is so different from the French way of working. The Japanese preferred to work in the same room as their boss. There was therefore no privacy on the part of the employee and everything is very formalized. In the French system, the boss will often have his/her own office and direct supervision of the employee was virtually non-existence. Employee-boss relationships are also less formal compared to the Japanese system and thus offer the employee a sense of freedom. For French persons is this way more relax and less stressful. The language problem presented an obvious problem in communication between employees of the two companies. However in the beginning there was a communication gap at different levels that prevented direct communication with employees of the respective firms. There was also less effective communication of the alliance and its meaning from top management to other employees. But they improved the communication through the common language (English), trainings and a clear system. All decisions are transparent and they need not many demands. These measures changed the behavior of the employees and the motivation increased also.

Figure 6: *Multiple cause diagram*

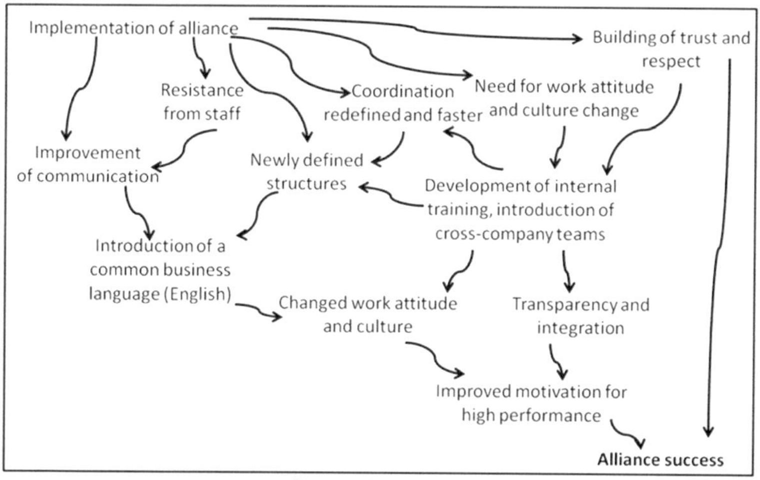

Source: Own figure.

In order to build trust and to increase the motivation and the alliance performance, Renault and Nissan have been committed to develop personnel exchanges since the beginning of the Alliance. Realizing the difficulties resulting form different languages and culture, they develop a special program to facilitate learning and familiarization of the operations and working culture of both companies. The issue of trust and mutual respect played a critical role in the formation of the alliance. At this time Nissan was facing financial difficulties of the alliance and urgently needed a bailout, the people at Renault did not see Renault as Nissan's rescuer and therefore the superior of the two. They were more willing to view the alliance as more balanced and complementary than imbalanced. There is no question of who is better than the other.

## Conclusion

The economic and financial results of the Renault-Nissan alliance are obvious. The deal contributed to Nissan revival and to Renault financial figures, increased profit margin and long term debt reduction. Both companies have increased in production, sales and market share. The following two figures show the growth.

Figure 7: *Production and sales*

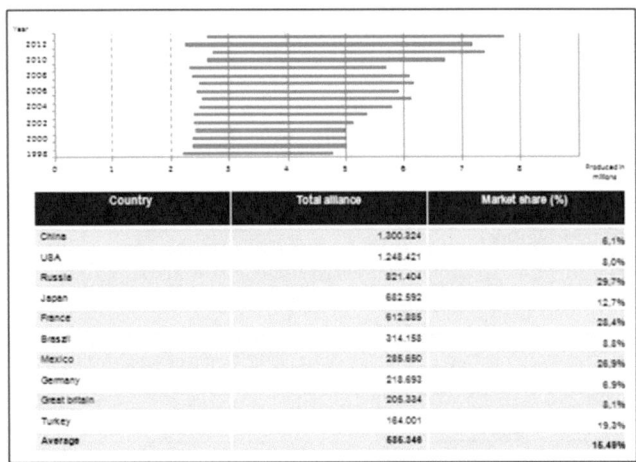

| Country | Total alliance | Market share (%) |
|---------|---------------|------------------|
| China | 1.300.324 | 6,1% |
| USA | 1.248.421 | 8,0% |
| Russia | 821.404 | 29,7% |
| Japan | 682.592 | 12,7% |
| France | 612.885 | 26,4% |
| Brazil | 314.158 | 8,8% |
| Mexico | 285.650 | 26,9% |
| Germany | 218.693 | 6,9% |
| Great britain | 205.334 | 8,1% |
| Turkey | 164.001 | 19,3% |
| Average | 586.346 | 15,49% |

Source: Own figure based on www.nissan-global.com, 2015; www.renault.com, 2015.

Figure 8: *Global market share in 1998, 2008 and 2010*

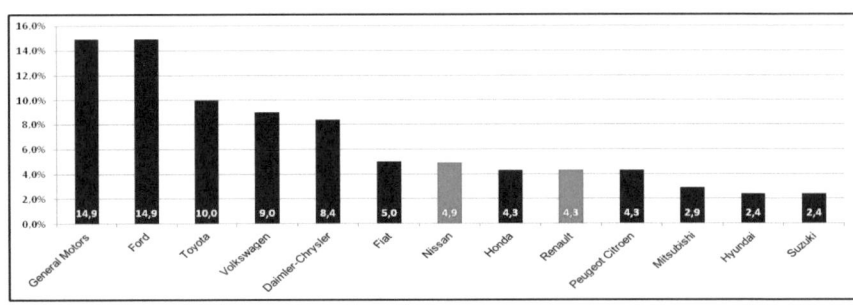

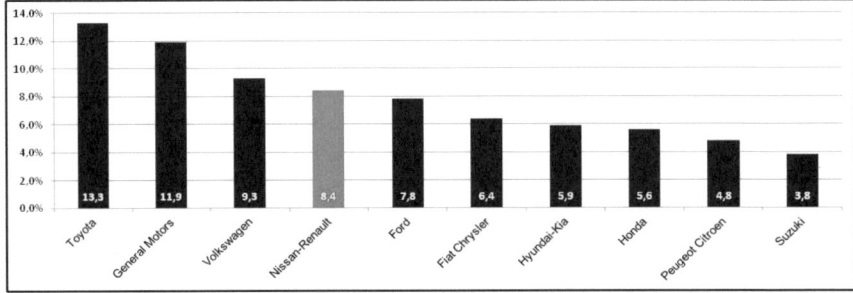

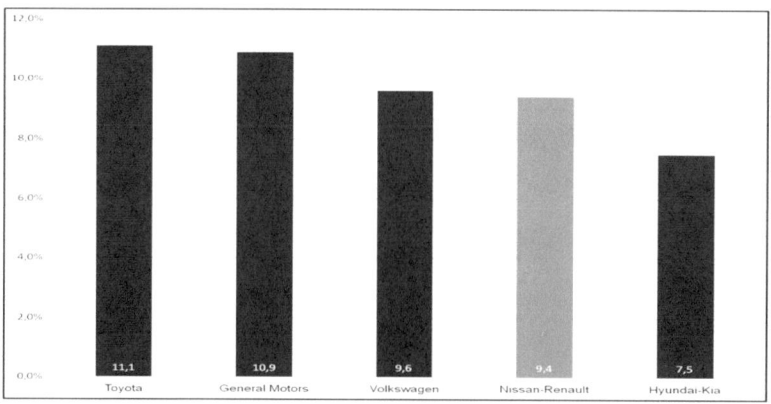

Source: Own figure based on www.nissan-global.com, 2015; www.renault.com, 2015.

Both companies, hence, the alliance have witnessed profitability and sales growth for the past and in 2010 they were the 4th largest automobile manufacturer in the world. Besides they improved their profitability and improved each other without losing their brand identity. Also it is obvious that Nissan`s management accepted to share Renault`s competencies in global strategic management, international finance and innovative-aggressive design instead of resisting to change on these issues. Within the management and total quality management of Renault would be particularly inspired by Nissan practices.

The basic reason for the success was the mutual trust, respect and communication. Furthermore the alliance is very transparency and they take decisions always very quickly and clearly (no misunderstandings). Based on these findings the pyramid of success has been developed.

Figure 9: *The pyramid of success of the alliance*

Source: Own figure.

# References

Arino, A., Garcia-Canal, E. & Valdes, A. (1999): "Longevity of strategic alliances between competitors: a dynamic value creation approach", Research Paper No 404, Online Link: http://www.iese.edu/research/pdfs/DI-0404-E.pdf, (01.April 2015).

Bamford, J., Ernst, D. & Fubini, D.G. (2004): „Launching a world-class joint venture", Harvard Business Review, 90-100, Online Link: http://hbr.org/2004/02/launching-a-world-class-joint-venture/ar/1, (01.April 2015).

Chanaron, J.J. (2007): "Globalization: How strategic alliances bring production and market advantages. The case of Renault/Nissan", TII Annual Conference, Gatehead-Newcastle Hilton.

Emerson V., (2000). "An Interview with Carlos Ghosn, President of Nissan Motors" And Industry Leader of the Year, Automotive News.

Fagan, P.L. & Yoshino, M.Y. (2003). "The Renault-Nissan Alliance", Harvard Business Schooll, Case Study.

Kale, P. & Singh, H. (2009): „Managing strategic alliances: what do we know now, and where do we go from here?, Vol. 23, No. 3, Online Link: http://connection.ebscohost.com/c/articles/43479263/managing-strategic-alliances-what-do-we-know-now-where-do-we-go-from-here, (01.April 2015).

Ring. P.S. (2000). "The three T´s of alliance cretion. Task, Team, and Time", European Management Journal, 18(2), No.2.pp.152-163.

Susini, J.P. (2004). "The Determinants of Alliance Performance: case Study of Renault & Nissan Aliance", Economic journal of Hokkaido University, 33, 232.262.